presented to

SMYTHE GAMBRELL LIBRARY

WESTMINSTER SCHOOLS

by

Bill Oglesby

1972

S.C.

# The FIRST BOOK of

# ANCIENT GREECE

BY
## Charles Alexander Robinson, Jr.

PICTURES BY
## Lili Réthi

FRANKLIN WATTS, INC.
575 Lexington Avenue, New York 22

For my Grandchildren

SBN 531-00463-5

*Library of Congress Catalog Card Number:* 60-5570

COPYRIGHT © 1960 BY FRANKLIN WATTS, INC.
Printed in the United States of America by
The Garrison Corp.

11    12

# CONTENTS

MACEDONIA

Mt. Olympus

SCYROS

IONIAN

SEA

CORCYRA

LEUCAS

CEPHALLENIA

ZACYNTHOS

Delphi

Thebes

Athens

PELOPONNESUS

Corinth

Olympia

Sparta

MELOS

CYTHERA

C      R

## THE LAND AND THE PEOPLE

IN southeastern Europe, jutting into the Mediterranean Sea,
is the mountainous peninsula called Greece. It is a small country — only 51,182 square miles in area, which is about the
size of New York State. The highest mountain in Greece is
Mount Olympus, which rises 9,570 feet above sea level. The
Greeks of long ago believed that the immortal gods lived on
Mount Olympus.

Greece is a beautiful country. The brilliant sunshine often makes the mountains look purple. The coast line is so broken that the deep blue sea seems to be everywhere. In the Aegean Sea, the part of the Mediterranean that lies east of Greece, there are many islands.

Twenty-five hundred years ago the people of this tiny, beautiful land developed the first democracy in history. This is an exciting thing to think about, especially when we remember that many countries in the world today have still not won self-government. Democracy began in Athens, the chief city of the part of Greece once called Attica, and the capital of Greece today.

In addition to developing democracy, the ancient Greeks produced beautiful art and literature. One very striking thing about them is that they believed in the importance and worth of the individual person. Another thing the Greeks believed was that men could discover the truth by using their brains. This was much better, they said, than following hunches and prejudices. The Greeks' respect for the individual and their belief in the power of men's minds were the chief reasons why they became the creators of what we call Western civilization — the civilization of the great democratic countries of the world.

*Theseus and the Minotaur*

## EARLY GREECE

THE Greeks came to Greece from central Europe about 2000 B.C. Because they used bronze as their chief metal, we call this very early time the Bronze Age.

There are many romantic legends about the Bronze Age. One tells of the Greek hero, Theseus, who sailed from Athens across the Aegean Sea southward to the island of Crete. There he slew a terrible human-headed bull called the Minotaur. The Minotaur was supposed to live in a huge underground stable called a labyrinth, full of twisting paths and tunnels where a man could lose himself and never find his way out. More than three thousand years later, beginning in 1900, the British archaeologist, Sir Arthur Evans, excavated at Knossos in Crete, where Theseus was supposed to have slain the Minotaur. Instead of a labyrinth, Sir Arthur found a beautiful palace that had belonged to King Minos. It is sev-

3

eral stories high and covers six acres. On the walls are bright paintings of men and flowers and birds.

Probably the most famous story of the Bronze Age is the story of the Trojan War. Troy was a city in Asia Minor on the Asiatic side of the Hellespont, that narrow strait between European and Asiatic Turkey which today we call the Dardanelles. According to the story, Paris, son of the Trojan King Priam, went to visit Menelaus of Sparta in Greece. There he fell in love with Menelaus' wife, Helen, and carried her back to Troy.

Immediately the kings of Greece — Menelaus, Achilles, Ajax, Odysseus — banded together under Agamemnon, the mighty king of Mycenae, to bring back "the most beautiful woman in the world," as Helen was called.

For ten long years·the Greeks and Trojans fought outside the walls of Troy. The Greeks could not get inside the city, but neither could the Trojans drive them away. At last the Greeks defeated the Trojans by a clever trick. They built a huge wooden horse and left it in full view on the plain. Then they pretended to sail home.

When the Greeks left, the Trojans came out of their city to look at the strange animal more closely. Near it they found a single Greek soldier who told them that the horse was a sacrifice to the goddess Athena. Believing that the horse would bring them luck, the Trojans decided to drag it inside

5                *The Trojan Horse*

their city. But the horse was so large that they had to tear down part of their walls in order to bring it in.

What the Trojans did not guess was that some Greek warriors had hidden themselves in the belly of the wooden horse. That night the warriors crept out. Their companions who had pretended to sail away returned and rushed through the hole in the walls to capture the city.

This was supposed to have happened in 1184 B.C., not long after the end of the Bronze Age. About four hundred years later the famous Greek poet, Homer, wrote about a part of the Trojan War. He called his long poem the *Iliad,* and in it he told how Achilles, the best of Greek warriors, lost his temper and stayed angrily in his tent until finally his dearest friend, Patroclus, was killed. He ended his poem with the death of Hector, the great Trojan hero, who was slain by Achilles.

Homer also wrote another poem called the *Odyssey.* It tells how the sly Odysseus wandered for ten years on his way home to Ithaca from Troy. His faithful wife, Penelope, waited for him all that time. On his long way home Odysseus, or Ulysses, as the Romans later called him, had all kinds of adventures. Among the strange people he met were the enchantress Circe, who turned his men into animals, and a one-eyed giant called Cyclops.

These, then, are some of the legends about early Greece. Once they were looked upon as myths, without any back-

*Achilles with the body of Hector*

ground of historical fact. But Heinrich Schliemann changed all that. He was a German-born businessman and archaeologist who spent many years of his life studying the places mentioned in the great poems of Homer. He believed that there had really been a war between the Greeks and Trojans, and to prove it he excavated the city of Troy. He was the first person ever to excavate layer by layer, and his success was very great. He proved not only that there had been a city of Troy, but that there had really been a Bronze Age, too.

*Circe*

# AN AGE OF COLONIZATION

SOON after Homer's day, the whole area around the Aegean Sea became so crowded that many Greeks went out as colonists to find new homes. They went to the Black Sea and to various parts of the Mediterranean, especially to Sicily and southern Italy.

In their new lands, the colonists met many people who were not Greeks. Sometimes the colonists gave their own civilization to the people among whom they settled. But much more important was the fact that the Greeks got new ideas — often strange and exciting ideas — from the people they met. When, for example, they met Egyptians, they discovered that Egypt had a far more ancient civilization than Greece. They also discovered that the Egyptians were as happy and prosperous as themselves despite their all-powerful rulers and differences in religion, diet, and dress. Discoveries such as these caused the Greeks to change their narrow way of thinking of their own way of life as the best and only one.

# THE CITY-STATES OF GREECE

WHEREVER the Greeks went, they kept the same kind of government they had at home. This was the city-state. The Greek word for it is *polis,* from which we get the word "political." The city-state was a small community situated in a valley and cut off by mountains from its neighbors. It was completely free in its home and foreign affairs, but as time went on some city-states tried to dominate others and build empires.

The city-states of Greece developed various kinds of government. Sparta had a monarchy. It was a military state, and all life was strictly organized. This was because Sparta had many serfs — men bound to the soil and forced to obey the owner of the land. The Spartans were so afraid the serfs would revolt that they had little time for the ways of peace. Corinth, on the other hand, was ruled by an aristocracy — by "the best," as the nobles were called. Athens had self-government. Its democracy was not exactly like ours, but the important point was that the people ruled themselves and did not have to answer to kings or nobles.

But no matter what type of government a city-state might have, the civilization throughout Greece was pretty much the same. More and more the Greeks came to look upon themselves as one people. The poems of Homer gave them a common background of history, and so did the statues of gods and heroes which artists carved. The Greeks had a common language and alphabet, too.

They also had common meeting places. One was Olympia, the home of the Olympic games. There, in 776 B.C., the famous games were started. They were held every four years with special magnificence. The competitive spirit of the games — in foot and chariot races, wrestling, and boxing — had a strong influence on all of Greek life.

Olympia was located in the Peloponnesus (southern Greece) and was sacred to Zeus, the father of gods and men. Zeus was the chief of all the gods, and in time the most intelligent Greeks looked upon him as the only god.

The second meeting place, Delphi, is still very beautiful. It is perched on a shelf of Mount Parnassus, the legendary home of the Muses — the goddesses of the nine arts and sciences. Overhead rise sharp cliffs, while below lies the Corinthian Gulf with the mountains of the Peloponnesus beyond, snow-capped except in the hottest months.

*Chariot race*

*Greeks consulting the oracle at Delphi*

12

At Delphi was a popular oracle. An oracle was the means — such as a priest or priestess — through which a god was supposed to talk to men. The oracle at Delphi was sacred to Apollo, the protector from evil, and god of Greek civilization itself.

The main purpose of an oracle was to give good, sound, everyday advice. The oracle at Delphi urged the Greeks to colonize the Mediterranean, which would relieve overcrowding at home. The oracle also urged the Greeks to free their slaves, because slavery was a black mark on their civilization.

Sometimes, though not often, an oracle looked into the future. When this happened, the clever priests tried to play it safe in order to be right.

When Croesus, a fabulously wealthy king in Asia Minor, was threatened by the Persians, he sent to Delphi to find out what might happen. He was told that a great empire would fall. He thought this referred to the Persian Empire, but it was his own that fell.

On another occasion, when the Persians were ready to invade Greece, the Athenians asked the oracle what to do. They were told to put their faith "in their wooden walls." Some thought this meant the wooden palisade around the Acropolis, and these men were killed when the Persians attacked and took the Acropolis. Others, fortunately, said that the oracle had meant the wooden bottoms of their ships, and in fact it was through their navy that the Athenians won.

13

Common gods as well as common meeting places made the Greeks feel like one people. The chief gods — such as Zeus, his wife-sister Hera, and Poseidon, the god of the sea — were worshiped by all Greeks. Each city-state also claimed one god as particularly its own, for the Greeks felt very close to their gods. The special deity at Athens was Athena, the goddess of wisdom and truth, the patron of the arts and sciences.

Zeus

Minerva

14

*Athene (from the Vatican Gallery at Rome)*

Apollo (from the Belvedere Gallery
    in the Vatican at Rome)

Venus

Poseidon

## THE RISE OF ATHENS

FOR a long time Athens was far less important than many other city-states in Greece. In 594 B.C., however, things started to change rapidly. In that year the Athenians asked a fellow citizen, a wise lawgiver named Solon, to make it possible for them to have a fuller voice in their government. Solon did this by putting all the citizens into an Assembly, which then elected the magistrates, or government officials.

Solon also decided to turn Athens from a farming community into one that might grow rich and important by manufacturing. Athens was fortunate in having fine natural resources — not only the marble of Mount Pentelicus, but also the silver mines of Laurium, and the wonderful clay in the Plain of Attica, which made possible the manufacture of beautiful vases. The important point for history, however, is that in order to make Athens a center of manufacturing, Solon had

16

to find his workmen abroad. Athens did not have enough potters and manufacturers of such things as shields and jewelry. In order to persuade outsiders to come to Athens, Solon knew he would have to promise them citizenship.

This does not sound strange or exciting to us, since our own country has been built up by immigrants. But in ancient Greek thinking, you had to be born in a state to be a citizen of that state. You had to be the free son of parents who had been born there.

Solon persuaded his fellow Athenians to let foreigners come to Athens, settle there, and become citizens. This broad-minded thinking helps to explain why Athens soon became the leading city of Greece.

17

*Solon persuading the Athenians to admit the foreigners*

# THE PERSIAN WARS

IT was lucky for Greece that Athens grew in power, for in less than a century the entire country was faced by Persian invasion. Eastward, from Asia Minor to India for a distance of 2,700 miles, stretched the mighty Persian Empire. Each Persian king tried to leave his son a larger state than he himself had inherited from his father.

This brings us to the opening of the fifth century, B.C., the most glorious century in the history of Greece. Since the Persians had conquered the Greek cities in Asia Minor, they now turned their eyes on Greece itself. In 490 B.C., Darius the Great, King of Persia, sent a fleet across the Aegean Sea from Asia Minor against Athens.

The Athenians, looking for help, sent a messenger to Sparta. The Spartans, however, did not want to risk a battle with the Persians and pretended that they had to wait till the full of the moon. And so when the Persians landed near Athens, on the Plain of Marathon, the Athenian general, Miltiades, and his Athenian troops were all alone. Nevertheless, they beat the Persians decisively in a bloody battle, and for the moment Greece was saved. We learn all this from the "History of the Persian Wars" by Herodotus (484-425 B.C.). Herodotus is called "the Father of History," because he was the first Greek ever to write a long history.

19 *Battle of the Greeks and Persians*

*Route of the Persians in the Bay of Salamis*

After the defeat of the Persians, enthusiasm at Athens ran high. The Athenians, urged on by another general, Themistocles by name, started to build a fleet. And the Spartans said they would fight if the Persians came again.

In 480 B.C., the Persians under their new king, Xerxes I, set out by land and sea along the northern Aegean coast for Greece. Leonidas I, the brave Spartan king, tried to stop them at the narrow pass of Thermopylae. Everyone with him was killed, but they made such a heroic stand that poets wrote about it afterward. The Persians then went on to Athens. There, in the Bay of Salamis, the Athenian fleet under Themistocles completely routed them, and the survivors retreated to Asia.

The victory meant that Greece — and with it, European civilization — had been saved from Asiatic conquest. It meant, too, that the people of Athens were full of confidence and enthusiasm, full of pride in their accomplishment. They were sure of themselves and their ability to mold the future as they wished. Many other Greeks were also proud of them.

# THE ATHENIAN EMPIRE

NO ONE could be absolutely certain, however, that the Persians would not come again. So, when Athens invited other Greek states to join in defense against Persia, many accepted. In Asia Minor, the Greeks whom Athens had just freed from Persia were anxious to join. So were the Greeks of the islands, since a new Persian fleet could pick the tiny islands off one by one.

That is how the Athenian Empire began. The head of it was Athens, but the empire itself stretched across the Aegean Sea to Asia Minor. To protect the empire, a large fleet of ships was necessary, and since the fleet depended on its rowers, the poorest citizens in the state, the poorest people of Athens were in some ways the most important. Therefore, they had an important voice in the government, and they strongly favored a government that ruled in their interest. In short, they supported democracy.

*Greek ship*

# PERICLES AND ATHENIAN DEMOCRACY

THE man chiefly responsible for making Athens great was a noble named Pericles. He was elected one of the chief magistrates at Athens almost every year from 461 B.C. until his death in 429 B.C. Since he held office so long, he was bound to influence governmental policy, and he believed that the people should rule themselves and have the benefit of an empire.

Every member-state of the Athenian Empire had to pay money to Athens for protection against a possible war with Persia or some other enemy. At first there was little objection to this, because Athens spent most of the money on the fleet, which did keep the Persians at a distance. The money that was left over, Athens spent as she wished.

The city of Athens was five miles from the sea, with a stone fortification wall around it, about twenty feet high. Since an enemy's army might starve the city into surrender, Pericles connected Athens with its harbor, Piraeus, by two long stone walls more than five hundred feet apart. Now, as long as the Athenian fleet ruled the Aegean Sea, food could be landed at Piraeus in time of war and brought up to Athens between the new long walls.

Athens had a population of about a quarter of a million people. Most of them were citizens and their families. Some were foreigners who lived in Athens for business reasons but did not seek citizenship. There were also some slaves, but the

*Athens and Piraeus*

Greeks never had masses of slaves. The slaves worked with their masters on the farms or in the shops and could look forward to being free someday — except those unfortunate slaves who were worked like animals in the mines.

In the time of Pericles, trade and business flourished at Athens. The standard of living rose. Beautiful temples, such as the Parthenon, were built on the hill of Athens known as the Acropolis. The government gave its support to various festivals, including the drama.

There have been few moments in history as great as the Periclean Age. Life was exciting, creative, and inventive. The ordinary Athenian citizen got a tremendous education by taking part actively in public affairs. He had the responsibility of running Athens and also the empire of which Athens was the proud capital. In order to do this, the Athenian citizens met in their Assembly once every ten days. The Assembly was the foundation of their democracy. All free men over eighteen years of age were members of it.

Every year five hundred men were chosen from the Assembly to make up the Council. The job of the Council was to attend to the business of the state between meetings of the Assembly and to bring proposals before the Assembly at its next meeting.

The chief executive officials of Athens were the Ten Generals. This was the Board to which Pericles was elected year after year. The Ten Generals were much more than military leaders. They carried out the various decisions of the Council and Assembly. They also met foreign envoys and supervised the numerous officials, such as those in charge of collecting the taxes and repairing the ships.

The right to be tried by your fellow men for a suspected crime is an important part of democracy. If this is lacking, then you may be in the grip of a dictator, or self-seeking noble, or prejudiced judge. Every year the Athenians selected five thousand citizens as jurors. These were then divided into smaller groups for the various cases.

*Pericles (from a bust in the British Museum, London)*

Every Athenian citizen in the days of Pericles felt that he helped run the government, that he had a stake in the future. With freedom and opportunity went responsibility. The Athenian who helped run his own government carried home with him a feeling of responsibility for his own and others' welfare that benefited not only government but every aspect of Athenian life.

27                     *The Acropolis*

# DAILY LIFE IN PERICLEAN ATHENS

LIFE in Athens, in the fifth century before Christ, was very simple. To understand it we must forget our complex life, our movies and autos and television, our huge factories. Periclean Athens was busy, but life was more informal and not as complicated as ours.

The family was a happy and devoted unit, but the father controlled it firmly. Women did not matter as much in society in those days as they do now. If they were respectable, they rarely appeared in public except for funerals, weddings, and festivals. The woman's job, so the Greeks believed, was running the home.

Girls received very little education. Boys were luckier — if their parents were rich enough, that is — because they were taught in small groups by educated Greek slaves. Mathematics was considered important, but the chief thing a boy studied was the poems of Homer. In these poems he learned about the heroes of the past, and the gods. An ambitious Athenian boy would also study public speaking, for this would help him get elected to office. Before that could happen, however, he had to serve in the army or navy for two years after reaching his eighteenth birthday.

The warm climate of Athens made living out-of-doors especially pleasant. For that reason, Athenian men looked on a dwelling more as a house than a home. They left their houses early in the morning for work or relaxation.

On most days the average Athenian worked at his job. His daily bread was his chief concern. He might be a farmer, cultivating vineyards and wheat fields or looking after olive trees. Or perhaps he was a skilled worker, making useful articles such as cups and mirrors. Other Athenians were shepherds and fishermen. Still others were engaged in trade and commerce.

Life, though simple, was active. After all, Athens was the head of an empire, and her people were constantly aware of a large world. Since Athens did not spend on the fleet all the money paid in by the members of the empire, the surplus money was used for the benefit of the citizens. Stone masons working on new temples and public buildings were paid with money from the empire.

The typical Athenian house rose beside a narrow, crooked street. There were almost no windows facing the street, just the door. Inside, life centered around a courtyard. This was open to the sky, and had flowers and bushes in it. Columns held up a roof on the sides, which gave protection against rain and sun. It was in the colonnade or open courtyard that Athenians talked and talked, and there was nothing they enjoyed so much. The various sleeping and living rooms were arranged around the courtyard, and only occasionally was there a second story. The chairs and tables and other furniture, like the house itself, were simple.

Athenian houses were made of sun-dried bricks, which washed away little by little in the rain. When a house collapsed, as Greek houses often did, everything in it would be buried. Then, instead of carting away the debris, the Athenian leveled it off and built another house on top of it. Over the years, a mound would slowly rise — a sure sign to a modern archaeologist where to excavate to find relics of Ancient Greece.

On the ordinary day when he had no special work to do, the average Athenian rose early and put on his short, woolen garment, called a *chiton*. He had some bread and wine for his

*The Agora, civic center of Athens*

breakfast and then, accompanied by a slave, went off to do the shopping. The men enjoyed doing this.

The Athenians had special market places for various things. They could not go to a supermarket or department store and do most of their shopping. If they wanted a bronze bowl, they went to the metal market. They bought fish at the fish market, oil at the oil market. Barber shops provided them news and gossip; water clocks and sundials told the time.

The Athenian man usually had his lunch and dinner at home with his family. Cheese, bread, and olives were eaten regularly because lamb and other meat were too expensive for most people. Green vegetables in season were popular. Fish was very popular, too, especially fish imported from the Black Sea. The food was cooked in the kitchen over a wood fire, and the various utensils, such as the frying pans and kettles, resembled ours. Either the woman of the house or a slave cooked and served the meals.

After a light lunch, the Athenian might spend the afternoon in a gymnasium, where he wrestled, boxed, and ran. And almost always there was the opportunity for serious discussion.

If an Athenian wished to entertain friends, he usually invited them home for dinner in the evening. During dinner, the men leaned back on couches. As soon as the meal was finished, those present decided on a topic to be discussed. Plato, the philosopher, tells us how his teacher, Socrates, was particularly welcome at dinner parties because he was able to talk so sensibly.

Much of the official business of Athens, such as the meetings of the Council and the worship of the gods, took place in the Agora. It was the civic center of the city. In it were some of the most important buildings of Athens — the Council House, the law courts, the mint, arsenal, and library, not to mention a music hall, temples, and colonnades.

*Athenian at dinner*

*The Parthenon*

## PHIDIAS AND ART

WHAT you notice first in Athens, today as in the past, is the Acropolis, which means "city height." The Acropolis at Athens is a low, broad hill. Originally it was a fort, but Pericles, a lover of all that was beautiful, decided to cover the hill with the finest temples Greek architects could build.

When you stand on the Acropolis today, you look out across the city to the Plain of Attica, which has always been filled with olive trees, and away to the mountains and the sea. But when you turn back to the Acropolis itself, you are chiefly struck by the marble temples round about you. The most famous of these is the Parthenon. It was sacred to the city's patron deity, Athena the Virgin ("Athene Parthenos" in Greek, from which comes the word "Parthenon").

Ictinus was the architect of the Parthenon. Phidias was its sculptor and, moreover, was the man Pericles appointed as the general artistic supervisor of the new buildings being put up. Phidias is regarded as the greatest artist of that day.

The most conspicuous thing about the Parthenon, or any Greek building, is the columns. These stand on a platform which is "crowned," as architects express it. For example, when you go to the Parthenon, put your hat on the corner of a step that leads up to the platform. Then run to the other end, bend down to the step and try to see your hat. You can't! The reason for this is that the steps rise slightly from each corner toward the center. Since the center is higher than the corners, you are unable to see your hat.

There was an artistic reason for this, and it helps to explain why the Parthenon has been hailed through the centuries as a model of perfection. If the steps and platform did not rise from corner to center (if they were not "crowned"), the whole thing would appear to dip in the middle. So the architect corrected the optical illusion by the crowning, which made the building appear full of strength and life.

*Parthenon steps, showing "crowning"*

The Parthenon had 17 columns along the sides, 8 each along the front and rear. This is a great many columns. But it was a big building, as Greek buildings go, about 228 feet long, 101 feet wide, and 65 feet high.

All of the Parthenon was made of marble, brought in from the quarries of Mount Pentelicus. An extraordinary fact about this marble is that it contains a good deal of iron. The iron gives off a golden glow against the white of the marble.

Greek architects invented three "orders" of architecture, as they are called: Doric, Ionic and Corinthian. These names refer to different kinds of columns and other details or decorations. The Parthenon represents the Doric order of architecture. Another fact about all Greek buildings is that many of the details were painted. Red, blue, yellow, and green were popular colors.

Doric          Ionic          Corinthian

*West pediment of the Parthenon*

One of the most beautiful things about the Parthenon was its sculpture. Greek sculpture portrayed men at their best; it idealized them. Sometimes when you look at a statue, you cannot be sure whether it is a statue of a man who appears like a god, or of a god who is very human. Another thing about Greek sculpture is its simplicity. Finally, it is full of strength.

The statues of the Parthenon showed Greek sculpture at its best. Some stood above the columns in the pediments or triangular gables at each end of the temple. Others stood elsewhere in the temple. Today many of the Parthenon sculptures are in the famous British Museum in London. They were taken there by Lord Elgin during the last century, when Greece belonged to Turkey.

The sculptures in the east pediment of the Parthenon — over the main entrance — represent the birth of Athena.

*East pediment of the Parthenon*

According to the story, Athena sprang fully armed from the head of Zeus. The sculptures in the west pediment show how Athena and Poseidon strove against each other to be chosen as the patron god of Athens. In this way, Phidias suggested to the beholders that the gods were particularly interested in Athens.

These great sculptures are "in the round" — this means that if you were strong enough, you could put your arms around them and lift them. Other sculptures on the Parthenon are in "relief" — that is, they rise from the background of the blocks from which they are carved. The sculptures in relief form a frieze, or procession. They show the best young men of Athens on horseback at the time of a great August festival. Other young men, and girls, too, are bringing animals to the sacrifice and various offerings to Athena.

The Parthenon — the architecture with its fine proportions, and the many sculptures of gods and idealized men — tells us a great deal about the people of ancient Athens. We see what they admired and held up as ideals. The Athenians, like other Greeks, were devoted to their state and its gods. Therefore, the Parthenon glorified both state and gods. It was a monument to civic patriotism and to religion as well.

Naturally, a period such as Periclean Athens produced many great artists. A fellow citizen of Phidias was Myron. He is famous for his statue of the *Discus Thrower,* a young athlete shown in a split second of rest. His arm has just gone back and in a moment will go forward and throw the discus, a circular plate of stone or metal which Greek athletes threw to test their strength. This statue is not only a fine piece of art, it also serves to remind us that the Greeks liked competitive sports and were interested in healthy bodies.

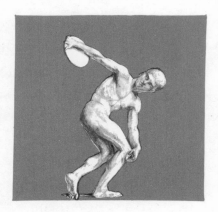

*Discobolus (Discus-thrower), by Myron*

*Sculpture of a Greek actor*

## SOPHOCLES AND THE DRAMA

THE Athenians had many festivals throughout the year —
athletic, religious, and civic. Most of them were put on by the
state itself, and in these the finest talent of Athens performed.
Other festivals were presented by small subdivisions of the
state. Almost every Athenian looked upon himself as an ex-
pert in festival performance, just as Americans who grew up
on baseball, dare watch the World Series and criticize the
playing!

39

The most important festival was the one given at Athens every spring. It lasted about a week, because there were several processions and dances by groups, and a large number of dramas, both tragic and comic. The center for all this was the theater of Dionysus. Dionysus was the god of wine and vegetation, of new birth and gladness, and of the theater.

The theater of Dionysus at Athens was on the south slope of the Acropolis. It was open to the sky. The auditorium had stone seats and held about 18,000 persons. At its bottom was a circular area, called the orchestra, and here in the orchestra all the action took place. Beyond the orchestra was a long building which served as background. The building was called "skene" in Greek, from which we get our word "scene."

The plays were produced at a time of religious celebration. For that reason, an altar sacred to Dionysus was placed in the center of the orchestra. On the steps of the altar sat the musicians, for there was much singing and dancing in a Greek play.

The performers were of two kinds. There were three professional actors who took the various roles. (If a play had more than three characters, an actor had to play more than one part.) The actors, men for both the male and female roles, were paid by the state. They wore masks with mouths shaped like megaphones to make themselves heard, though Greek theaters had very good acoustics indeed.

The rest of the performers, fifteen men in number, made up the chorus. They both sang and danced. The chorus consisted of amateurs and was paid by a wealthy citizen who was appointed as producer by the state. This was a form of taxation, but it was not resented, because an official committee awarded prizes at the end of the week. They went to the best producer, the best actor, and the best dramatist. In other words, the spirit of the festival was highly competitive as well as religious.

*Theater of Dionysus, Athens*

The audience gathered not long after dawn on the appointed day and saw three tragedies in succession by one dramatist. The next two days, two more dramatists presented three tragedies apiece. Comedies were also given.

Greek tragedy, in general, is concerned first with man's worth and his individual responsibility. It deals with the problem of evil in this world. It teaches that our duty to God is higher than obedience to a bad government. The dramatists were, in a sense, the teachers of Athens.

Sophocles (496-406 B.C.), who was a great tragic poet, represents the Greek ideal that we must be both thinking and active men. In the year 443 B.C., Pericles appointed him chief treasurer of the Athenian Empire. Three years later, having meanwhile produced his great drama, *Antigone,* Sophocles served as general in a war. When it came to writing dramas, this man of action was chiefly interested in what effect experience had upon a man's character and soul.

One of Sophocles' plays, *Oedipus the King,* has an extraordinary story to tell about Thebes, an ancient city in central Greece. An oracle had once informed Laius and Jocasta, the king and queen of Thebes, that a son born to them would murder his father and marry his mother.

Terrified by such an awful prophecy, the parents gave their young son, Oedipus by name, to a slave, with orders to leave him to die on a nearby mountain.

Not wanting to abandon the baby, the slave brought him to

Corinth. When Oedipus grew up, some of his friends teased him about his birth. So Oedipus jumped into a boat, sailed across the Corinthian Gulf to Delphi, and asked the oracle about himself. The oracle told him that he would murder his father and marry his mother.

Oedipus hurried off in the opposite direction from Corinth as fast as he could. At a spot where three roads came together, he met an elderly man in a chariot, with several servants. There was an argument about the right of way — a fight followed, and the younger man slew the elder. Without realizing it, Oedipus had killed his father.

When he reached Thebes, Oedipus found that a terrible plague had fallen on the city. An oracle had said that the plague would remain until the riddle of the Sphinx was guessed. The riddle was, "What is it that walks on four legs in the morning, two at midday, and three in the evening?" Oedipus guessed that it was man (because we go on all fours early in life, and when we get old, we may use a cane).

*Oedipus and the Sphinx*

The Sphinx fell over, and the plague disappeared. The Thebans in joy and gratitude made Oedipus their king. And then he married Jocasta, the widow of the late king. He did not know that this was his mother. The years passed, and they had children.

By the end of the play, Jocasta has killed herself, and Oedipus has torn out his eyes. Oedipus, however, conducts himself so nobly under all this stress that feelings of pity and fear are aroused in us. In fact, we are overwhelmed by the tragedy of a man who is powerless in the face of forces greater than himself. These emotions seem to purify our minds — to make us more sympathetic toward others and less harsh in our judgments.

Just as Phidias was by no means the only great artist, so Sophocles was surrounded by dramatists as great as himself. One such tragic poet was Aeschylus, another was Euripides, while the outstanding comic poet was Aristophanes. With these poets, Greek drama reached heights that have never been equaled except by Shakespeare.

## SOCRATES AND PHILOSOPHY

BEFORE the time of Pericles, the Greeks had been much interested in science, even though they could not carry their scientific studies very far because they lacked precise instruments.

*Socrates*

But with the rise of democracy and its ideals of human equality, the ordinary man had become important. It was natural that Periclean Athens should turn to the study of the nature of man himself.

Socrates (470-399 B.C.) was the great example of the new attitude, of the new interest in man. He was a poor Athenian, full of loyalty and love for his country and his fellow citizens. He loyally performed his duties as a soldier and as a member of the Assembly.

Socrates was "a lover of wisdom," a philosopher. In his pursuit of knowledge, he spent long hours just thinking. He

45

wanted to discover the truth. He particularly wanted to know what people meant by God and the immortality of the soul, by beauty and justice and democracy and their opposites. He tried to find out what is the best way for men to live and behave.

It seemed to Socrates that the gods were everywhere and knew everything. As he looked at the world, he felt that the world had been made for men. He said that there was a grand design visible, which could only be due to the wisdom of the gods, or as he preferred to say, to God. Socrates reasoned that since man is capable of good, God must have made him. Therefore, he added, the best of human practices and societies are the most God-fearing.

Socrates was forever on the move around Athens, often going where the crowds were thickest. His method was to stop people and ask questions. When he got his answer, he asked another question and so on. He pretended ignorance on all things himself. But he kept asking more questions and soon proved that his acquaintances knew less than he. In this way, he prepared them to listen while he gave his own definitions of such things as courage and beauty.

The Athenians eventually put Socrates on trial for his life. They said that he was encouraging young men to revolt against the state and the ancient gods. The charges were false, but the Athenians had recently lost a long war with Sparta and were tired. They were tired, too, of a man who was forever asking questions and seeking the truth. Socrates was condemned to death. While he was in prison, he had the chance to escape, but he said that he would not break the law. When a friend asked him how he wished to be buried, he replied that they could put his body anywhere at all, but they could never catch his immortal soul. He declared that he was going to a place where no harm could come to anyone. As was the custom in Athens, his jailer brought him a cup of poison hemlock. Socrates took it from the weeping jailer's hands, drank it quietly, and died.

Socrates never wrote a word. We learn about him from various pupils, the most famous of whom was the great Athenian philosopher, Plato (427-347 B.C.). Plato was a young man when Socrates was put on trial for his life, and was among the friends and pupils who crowded his jail cell while he died. Immediately afterward, Plato wrote an account of the trial and death of Socrates. His *Apology,* as it is called, gives the actual scene in the courtroom and is a glorification of a great man's life.

Not much later, Plato opened up a school for young men in his own home which he named "the Academy." He also wrote plays on philosophy. These are called "dialogues," because in each work various people join in discussing a particular topic. The main speaker is always Plato's revered master, Socrates. Probably the most important dialogue Plato ever wrote is the *Republic,* in which Socrates discusses the ideal state — its educational, social, and political forms.

Plato had a fine, creative mind. His chief virtue is that he makes us think hard concerning the topic under discussion. His most famous pupil, the philosopher Aristotle (384-322 B.C.), was different. Aristotle was really a teacher who, instead of asking questions, gave knowledge. He wrote much on politics. He also studied physics and astronomy, psychology and physiology, zoology and botany.

Throughout ancient times people referred to Aristotle as if he were the last word on a subject. We cannot blame Aristotle for this, but we must criticize people who are unwilling to think for themselves. Periclean Athens, however, did its own thinking. It rose to great heights because the Athenians insisted on challenging anything they wished. In this way, Phidias and Sophocles, Socrates and others, reached new ideas about man and nature and life itself.


## THUCYDIDES AND HISTORY

WE would expect Periclean Athens to produce great historians, just as it produced great philosophers, dramatists, and artists. History, in particular, grew up as a result of the eagerness to know the past of the human race. But since Periclean Athens was so deeply interested in the present, historians emphasized contemporary events.

The greatest Greek historian, Thucydides (471-399 B.C.), chose to describe the long war between Athens and Sparta that raged during his lifetime. This is known as the Peloponnesian War (431-404 B.C.), because the chief enemies of Athens — Sparta and Corinth — were located in southern Greece, in the Peloponnesus. The war ended with the overthrow of Athens.

Like other men of Periclean Athens, Thucydides was both a writer and a man of action. He served briefly as a general in the war and then turned to writing up its events. Thucydides is considered a great historian because he was absolutely fair in his story. He loved Athens, his native state, but he did not hesitate to criticize her.

Thucydides traveled around during the war and asked questions of people on both sides. In this way he got the whole picture. Then he used his tremendous intellectual power to dig down and see what forces were at work underneath it all. He found out that the war was caused by the fear that other Greeks had of Athens.

Athens had a large empire, her power was growing greater, and her democracy stood as a challenge to states governed by aristocracies or kings. Athens represented something new, and many people feared the new.

As the war went on, Thucydides studied its revolutions and atrocities. It was clear to him that love of power produced most of these evils. And he was shocked when his own city of Athens adopted the policy that "Might makes Right."

Pericles had died in 429 B.C., not long after the outbreak of the war. Then, unfortunately, Athens had poor leaders. The people were even persuaded to send an expedition westward across the Mediterranean Sea to try to capture a big Greek city on the island of Sicily, known as Syracuse. The whole Athenian expedition, both ships and men, was destroyed.

When, at last, the war ended with Athens' defeat, she had to give up her empire. This was also the end of the extraordinary fifth century B.C.

## ALEXANDER THE GREAT

ATHENS had tried to join together some of the Greek city-states in a union and had failed. The greatest failure of the ancient Greeks, as a matter of fact, was their unwillingness to unite and stop all their wars. Now it was done for them by a conqueror from Macedonia in northern Greece.

The conqueror of all Greece was a young man, Alexander the Great (356-323 B.C.). After his conquest of Greece, he marched east against the Persian Empire. He had 30,000 infantry and 5,000 cavalry, whereas the mighty Persian Empire had armies of 100,000 men and more. But Alexander was a military genius and never lost a battle. He marched as far as

*Alexander in India*

Danube R.

BLACK SEA

MACEDONIA

Byzantium

Granicus

PHRYGIA

Athens

Sparta

CRETE

ARMENIA

Issus

MESOPOTAMIA

Gaugam

Arbel

Euphrates

Tigris

MEDITERRANEAN SEA

Damascus

Babylon

Alexandria

LIBYA

Memphis

Ammon

R. Nile

ARABIAN DESERT

EGYPT

RED SEA

•••••• Alexander's route

ARAL
SEA

R.Jaxartes

MASSAGETAE

●Tashkend
●Alexandreschate

SOGDIANA

BACTRIA

CASPIAN SEA

PARTHIA

MEDIA

DRANGIANA

ARACHOSIA

Indus

R.Hydaspes

●Alexandria

Persepolis

Bampur

GEDROSIA

INDIA

PERSIAN GULF

Nearchus voyage

INDIAN OCEAN

*Alexander the Great (from a statue in the temple at Shami, Persia)*

India, and then turned back westward, but at Babylon, in Mesopotamia, he died of a fever.

The most important thing about Alexander is the idea he developed concerning the sameness of all people. He believed that the world was a unit and that all people were alike under their skins.

Because of Alexander's conquests, the new, large world east of Greece now took on one civilization — Greek. Or rather, the various peoples in it — such as the Egyptians and Syrians — kept their own ways and added Greek civilization as a sort of common bond. For example, even though Jesus and his disciples spoke a Semitic language, Aramaic, at home, the New Testament was written in Greek, so that everyone might understand it.

The new world, after Alexander's time, was made up of big kingdoms, not city-states. The most important of these was Egypt. The capital was Alexandria, which Alexander had founded and named for himself.

Alexandria had a population of a million persons. It was a busy, prosperous city. Great scholars and scientists worked in its libraries and museums. Some of them studied and wrote about Homer and the Greek dramatists. Euclid (323-285 B.C.) wrote a book on geometry that is so clear that little improvement has ever been made on it.

*Lighthouse in the harbor at Alexandria*

*Archimedes*

Archimedes (287-212 B.C.), another scientist, discovered, as he was getting into his bath one day, the relationship between weight and displacement of water — the principle of specific gravity, as it is called. He was so excited that he ran through the streets naked, crying, "Eureka, I have found it."

Perhaps the greatest Greek scientist was Aristarchus (about the third century B.C.). His estimate of the length of the year was only seven minutes and sixteen seconds too short. He also discovered that the earth goes around the sun. This is known as the heliocentric theory. Most people did not want to believe that our own planet was not the center of things, so they kept on believing in the geocentric theory, that the sun goes around the earth.

The new world which Alexander opened up to the Greeks and their civilization lasted for three hundred years. Then Rome, the great power westward in Italy, conquered it, and the whole ancient world was united in the Roman Empire.

*Roman Legions landing in Egypt*

*Apollo Sanroktonos (the Lizard Slayer)*

## THE LEGACY OF GREECE

THE Romans adopted a good deal of Greek civilization, just as the Egyptians and Syrians had done. Since much of modern Europe — such as England, France, and Italy — was carved out of the Roman Empire after its fall, the civilization of the Greeks, as well as the Romans, has been passed on to us.

One great thing we have inherited from ancient Greece is the idea about the importance and worth of the individual. We also believe, as the Greeks did, that we should seek the truth and be guided by it. We should be warned by them that war often leads to disaster, but that unity can produce peace and prosperity.

Much of Greek art is a joy to look at, it seems so perfect. Greek drama, philosophy, and other literature tell us about man and God and the meaning of life. But most important of all is the Greek idea of democracy, which allows all men to govern themselves.

# A FEW OF THE WORDS WE HAVE
# INHERITED FROM THE GREEKS

AMNESIA. Loss of memory. From the Greek *amnesia*, forgetfulness.

ANALYSIS. The separation of something into its parts; an examination to find out of what something is made. From the Greek *analusis*, a taking apart.

ANEMONE. Wind flower. From the Greek *anemos*, the wind. The Greeks believed that the anemone opened its petals only when the wind blew.

COSMOS. Order, harmony; the world, because of its orderliness. In Greek, *kosmos*.

CRANIUM. The skull, the head. In Greek, *kranion*.

DRAMA. A play. The Greek word is the same, derived from the Greek verb *dran*, to do, or act.

EMPHASIS. Special importance given to something. The Greek word is the same, derived from *en* (to) plus *phainein* (show).

GERANIUM. A flower also known as crane's bill. In Greek, *geranios*, from *geranos*, a crane.

HERCULEAN. Of great difficulty. From *Hercules*, the Greek hero who performed difficult and dangerous tasks.

HIPPOPOTAMUS. A large animal with hairless skin, living in African rivers. In Greek, *hippopotamos*, from *hippos* (horse) plus *potamos* (river). Literally, a river horse.

MUSEUM. A place for study, especially of the arts and sciences. From the Greek *Mouseion*, a temple of the Muses.

PARAPHERNALIA. Property, belongings, or equipment. From the Greek *parapherne*, derived from *para* (beside) plus *phrene* (dowry).

RHINOCEROS. A large, thick-skinned animal with one or two horns on its snout. In Greek, *rhinokeros*, from *rhinos* (the nose) plus *keros* (horn).

STIGMA. A mark of disgrace or reproach. In Greek, the same word means the prick or mark made by a pointed instrument.

SYMPATHY. The entering into and sharing the feelings, interests, or aims of another. In Greek, *sympatheia*, from *syn* (with) plus *pathos* (suffering).

# INDEX

60

61